THE
Archive Photographs
SERIES

LITTLEPORT

CORONATION WEEK, 1953. Part of a parade to start the celebrations leading up to the coronation of Queen Elizabeth II, which was held on Sunday 31 May 1953. Here we see the Womens Institute and Salvation Army, contingents of the parade, heading up High Street towards the open-air united service held in the grounds of Highfield House.

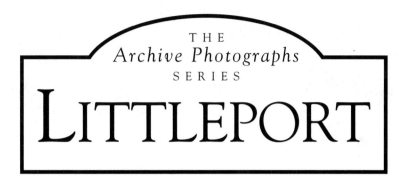

THE
Archive Photographs
SERIES

LITTLEPORT

Compiled by
The Littleport Society

CHALFORD

First published 1997
Copyright © The Littleport Society, 1997

The Chalford Publishing Company
St Mary's Mill, Chalford,
Stroud, Gloucestershire, GL6 8NX

ISBN 0 7524 1006 7

Typesetting and origination by
The Chalford Publishing Company
Printed in Great Britain by
Bailey Print, Dursley, Gloucestershire

Contents

Foreword

During the past sixty years the inevitable march of progress has swept away much of what was familiar to the older generations. Littleport has not escaped that change. It is, therefore, appropriate that as the century draws to its close a photographic record should be compiled. The task has been ably undertaken by David Porter and fellow members of the Littleport Society. I am pleased to commend to you *Littleport*, a fascinating collection of old postcards and photographs, that will, I am sure, be a treasured source of information and nostalgia for many years.

Roger Rudderham
Vice-President of the Littleport Society

Introduction

Littleport probably takes its name from the Latin word portus, meaning a landing place. In early documents the word appears as Littleport, Litelport, Lytleport or Lytilport.

Before the Fens were drained Littleport was a separate island, surrounded on all sides by Fens, meres and marshes. It was connected to the Isle of Ely by a causeway which was only passable in the summer months. The River Ouse followed a meandering course from Ely to Littleport, after changing course as the water found its own way over the marshes.

Before the fourteenth century when a channel was dug from Littleport Bridge to Denver, to divert the water to Kings Lynn, the river turned sharply at the spot where the bridge is now, came up Station Road, turned North West at Quay Hill and wandered over the Fens to Wisbech, which was then called Ousebridge. The words, the Hythe, which is a street in the village, means 'a place where boats are tied'. The river, now known as the Old Croft River, was navigable as far as Littleport for small ships bringing goods for Ely and the surrounding country. The river still plays a large part in the life of the village. Parties of people come from all over the country to fish in its waters. Pleasure craft based at the Boathaven, which used to be the docks, do a good trade and public houses, like the Black Horse, which stands at the foot of Sandhill Bridge, prosper serving meals as well as drinks. Years ago strings of barges plied up and down the river carrying sugar beet from the farms to the Beet Sugar Factory at Ely. Some of the barges came from Kings' Lynn bringing goods from the port there. Others collected vegetables of all kinds from the farms and delivered them to the docks at Littleport. The docks adjoined the railway yard and trucks were waiting to take the produce on its way.

Transport by road put an end to this river traffic and was partially responsible for doing away with Littleport station. People prefer to travel by car or bus which is more convenient. For those who still prefer the railway the electric trains still stop at Littleport's railway halt!

I remember that we made our own pleasure in my younger days. We could play out of doors then with no fear. There was no wireless or television, we had bicycles but there were no cars. If we needed to travel a distance we either cycled or went by horse and cart. A horse-drawn covered wagon used to take people to and from Ely market every Thursday for sixpence. Now there are frequent buses and nearly everyone has access to a car. For exercise we either walked or played tennis, badminton, cricket or football. Clubs for all these existed and there was a flourishing cycle club which was famous for miles around. The cyclists used to give displays and hold competitions on show days which were then held at High Field, as they are today. We also had a swimming club and members swam either in the river or at the swimming pool which was built on what was known as the Sheep Brook. The river was safe for swimming then, but is much too deep today.

People now have a beautiful new leisure centre on Camel Road with all the facilities anyone could need, both indoors and out, provided for them. This is indeed an amenity which was never dreamed of in my young days.

Littleport has never been an industrial centre. Its only factory for many years was Hope Brothers Shirt Factory built in 1881 by Thomas Peacock. This factory has changed hands two or three times over the years and is now a branch of Burberry's. The world famous Burberry raincoats are made there. Other factories and businesses have come to the Henry Crabb Industrial Estate during the past few years, a branch of Ede and Ravenscroft make robes for academics, Histon Concrete make pre-cast concrete structures of all kinds. Some of these are currently being used in the building of the new Centre Court at Wimbledon. Ernest Doe has an establishment on the estate too, this is an agricultural engineering firm. At the other end of the village there is a branch of J.D.R. which makes underwater cables which are used all over the world.

Many of the vegetables sent from the farms around Littleport to markets all over this country and Europe are washed and packed at Steven Layn's Packing Station on Woodfen. Many farms have their own washing equipment and transport but for others we have Murfitt's Transport, the Norfolk line. This firm has lorries which travel all over Europe carrying vegetables and fruit from Littleport's farms.

Littleport has been slow to change over the years. In medieval times life depended on fishing, catching wild fowl, gathering reeds for thatching and floor covering and generally trying to survive. After the Fens were drained people still depended upon the land for their livelihood. Water was controlled by rivers, canals and dykes so fields could be cultivated. Crops were grown and harvested and when I was young many people worked in the fields, planting, sowing, weeding and gathering in the harvest. Now machinery has taken the place of people and very few are now needed on the farms.

I have referred to the nature of the Fens around Littleport before they were drained. The drainage was carried out between 1600 and 1660, the chief engineer of the project was Cornelius Vermuyden, a Dutchman, called in by James I. He drew maps and made plans for what turned out to be a massive task. Unfortunately it was not entirely successful and flooding occurred on a fairly regular basis. In 1947, exactly fifty years ago, there was a very serious flood and nearly the whole of the area for miles around was under water. To prevent this happening again the Flood Protection Scheme was planned. This was carried out and has proved successful so far. It is an interesting and fascinating subject but far too long for an article of this description. Both the drainage of the Fens and the Flood Protection Scheme have been written about in books which can be obtained from libraries.

St George's church in the village gives a feeling of simplicity. It dates from the fifteenth century. The style is perpendicular although there are traces of early English architecture. There is evidence of some fourteenth century work and an older building. The church has some lovely stained glass windows and is well worth a visit.

When Littleport is mentioned the Littleport Riots spring immediately to mind. After the defeat of Napoleon at Waterloo in 1815 this country was left in a very poor condition. The rates and taxes raised to pay for the wars had rendered farmers and other employers too poor themselves to pay very much for labour. Hundreds of the very poor were starving. There was general dissatisfaction all over the country and this boiled over in Littleport on 22 May 1816 in the Globe Inn (now demolished) the rioters, angry and inflamed with drink ran riot. They broke into houses and shops in the Main Street, marched on the vicarage and generally caused mayhem. They then decided to march on to Ely where they caused more disruption before making their way back to Littleport. When they realised the Militia had been called from Bury St Edmunds they barricaded themselves in the George and Dragon public house. In the fight that followed, two men were shot many were arrested and committed for trial. Five were hanged, several were transported to Australia and some were imprisoned. Nearly every family in the village was affected in one way or another by the uprising. There is a very full and detailed account for this, too, in a book published locally.

E.R. Gill
June 1997

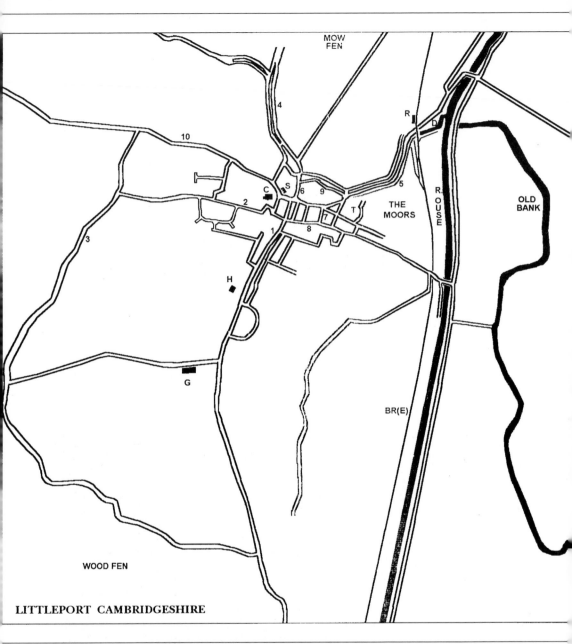

MOW FEN

THE MOORS

R. OUSE

OLD BANK

BR(E)

WOOD FEN

LITTLEPORT CAMBRIDGESHIRE

LITTLEPORT, 1947. This sketch map shows the road, rail and river layout of Littleport just after the Second World War. Note how 'Old Bank' and the series of parallel roads to the north of the village show the original course of the Ouse River before the river was diverted to Kings Lynn in the 1200s. Some of the places and roads portrayed in this volume are indicated as follows. C: the church, D: the docks, G: the Grange, H: Highfield House, R: railway station, S: the school, T: the Holmes, 1: High Street, 2: Parsons Lane, 3: Woodfen Road, 4: New Road, 5: Station Road and the Holmes River, 6: Ponts Hill, 7: Granby Street, 8: Main Street, 9: The Hythe, 10: Wisbech Road.

One
Parades and Shows

A PARADE IN THE EARLY 1900s. Riders on horses and donkeys pass Hope Brothers factory and Connie Cawthorne's general store at No.13 Victoria Street.

CORONATION PARADE, 31 May 1953. The Littleport Band heads the parade along High Street. On the left the Hovis sign was on Register's bakery shop at No.34 High Street, and on the right Snushall's fish and chip shop was in some cottages (at No.31 High Street) that have since been demolished. The Union Flag was on a pole in the garden of Knight House at No.25 High Street. The Littleport Band was followed by local dignitaries and then the British Legion.

CORONATION PARADE, 31 May 1953. The Salvation Army, the Littleport Womens Fellowship, the Red Cross and the St John's ambulance brigade. Note the cross on the peak of St John's Methodist church, which crashed onto the footpath in a gale in 1989. See also page 52.

HIGHFIELD, 31 May 1953. The Queen Elizabeth II Coronation Parade has arrived in the grounds of Highfield House. The Revd Canon J.K.C. Payne is officiating at the open air church service for all denominations on that Sunday afternoon.

CORONATION WEEK, 1953. Amongst the many events which took place in Littleport was this Soapbox Derby at Ponts Hill. Competitors are, from left to right: Tony Gipp, John Wilson (driver), John Coleby, Harry Coleby (driver), Norman Howe, Allan Barrett (driver), Alan Youngs and Tony Copsey (driver).

ARMISTICE PARADE, 1930. As on many similar occasions there is a boy on a bicycle beside the parade, another small boy in large wellington boots is marching alongside. In the background the iron railings and pile of bricks are all that remain of 'Audley House' (see page 61).

PARADE SUNDAY, 20 July 1952. Passing along Church Lane with No.1 'The Limes' on the right and No.8 'The Herons' on the left. The ladies of the Womens Institute are followed by their float which depicts some of their activities; music was portrayed by Mrs V. Everett and Mrs D. Kerridge of the choir, and cooking by Mrs D. Fendick and Mrs A. Norman.

HOSPITAL PARADE, *c.* 1910. Bill Collins is holding the head of the horse pulling this float collecting for Addenbrookes Hospital. The middle man of the three standing at the back is Ron Barber's father Charlie Barber, the driver is John Cross. Behind them is the YMCA hut, a typical 'army barracks building', which later housed the firm of Littleport Engineering. It was demolished in the 1970s.

SILVER JUBILEE, 1935. The parade, celebrating the Silver Jubilee of King George V and Queen Mary, passes into Granby Street from Station Road, which was formerly known as Ferry Lane. The building on the right is Brewery House, at No. 6 Granby Street, which is also mentioned on page 68. How many men would be wearing hats on a similar parade these days?

THE SECOND WORLD WAR SAVINGS. The 'Salute the Soldier' target board has a moving arm indicator to show total savings in Littleport during one wartime week. This is sited outside Wright's saddlers shop in Main Street, Albert Wright is seated on the left.

SPITFIRE FUND, 1940. The closing date of the County Spitfire Fund was 15 October. Littleport raised £1,691 5s 9d towards an aeroplane. At the Regal Cinema, Hempfield Road, on the steps, from left to right are: Mr Thurling, Mr 'Bif' Harrison, Mr Goy, Mr C.W. Flunder, Mr A.W. Wright, Mr Barrett, Mr Harley and Mr Self.

STREET PARTY, 1945. The victory party in 'The Crescent', one of the many parties to celebrate the end of the Second World War. A collection was made in each separate street, and the proceeds used for a party in that street. Any cash remaining was divided among those children, although this meant that some children received more than others, because some streets with many houses had only a few children!

GIRL GUIDES, 15 June 1950. Littleport Band leads local Girl Guides on a horse-drawn float carrying a scroll en-route to the first post-war World Guide Conference in Oxford. The overnight stop for the scroll was at the Globe Lane chapel. The Guider at the time was Margaret Martin.

ROYAL OCCASION, 1902. The Salvation Army band and a crowd on the corner of Main Street and Granby Street, then the main road from Kings Lynn to Cambridge. Laburnum Lodge with its ornate railings is in the background. The man in the centre appears to be reading a speech. This is thought to be part of the celebrations for Edward VII's Coronation.

FOUNDATION LAYING, 1890. This is believed to be the stone-laying ceremony of the Constitutional Hall, on 15 June 1890. There are six stones, but two of these are now indecipherable, the others name the stone layers as William Luddington, Joseph Martin JP, Capt. G.W. Selwyn MP and William Cutlack senior. The hall, which was finished in 1893, is now the Village Hall.

SUNDAY SCHOOL TREAT, 1897. This was held in Peacock's field, which is now Limes Close. It was a popular venue for 'treats' or outings of this kind. The children are posing in front of hired swings.

LITTLEPORT SHOW, 1950s. Business competitors battle it out on the greasy pole at the show, with Philip Dewey and Harold Gotobed, proprietors of Littleport's two hardware stores in friendly rivalry. Although Phil was destined for an early bath, he subsequently pulled Harold into the water.

Two
Sports and Pastimes

GASHOUSE GREEN, 1900s. No it's not a maypole! Volunteer firemen are hauling hoses up the pole to drain and dry. The horse-drawn fire engine is standing in front of the garage just to the left of the pole.

FENLAND SKATING PRINT. This print shows the race held in 1890 on the Great Ouse River near Arbers Mill (see also page 44). In the final, James Smart of Welney on the Cambridgeshire and Norfolk border, beat Tommy Wells of Isleham in Cambridgeshire.

SID GREENHALL, NATIONAL CHAMPION SKATER. Sid Greenhall from Landbeach, Cambridgeshire won the Littleport Challenge Cup in 1909, after winning the Professional Skating Championship of Great Britain in the previous year.

RESCUE FROM THE ICE, 1900. One of the hazards of skating on thin ice in the open air, as opposed to inside the arena, is that it can crack quite unexpectedly. Fortunately the water, on the deliberately flooded area of The Moors, was quite shallow, and this unfortunate fellow lost only his dignity and not his life before he was pulled out.

ICE MAIDENS SKATING, in the Ladies Race held on The Moors in 1895. Regrettably the names of the contestants have been lost. It is rather amusing to note the style of attire that a well-dressed female skater was expected to wear in those Victorian days! Skating was extremely popular in the village at this time, and there are twenty-four people on a photograph of Littleport Skating Club Committee dated 1895.

LITTLEPORT SKATING CHALLENGE CUP. Known as the Fifty Guineas Cup, it was made from 100 ounces of solid silver, and stood two feet and three inches in height. C. Brett was the winner in 1912, but for various reasons it was never raced for again. Sadly nobody seems to know what happened to this splendid trophy. The Moors were never deliberately flooded again after 1917.

LITTLEPORT SWIMMING CLUB, WATER SPORTS, 1914. For many years the Great Ouse River was the venue for this popular event. In the 1950s the barges, used as starting bases and judging platforms, were provided by the British Sugar Corporation.

CRICKET, 1894. The sound of leather on willow has echoed in Littleport for many years, during which time the various teams have met with varying degrees of success. Anyone born when this picture was taken, and still alive now, would be enjoying an innings of one hundred and three, not out!

CRICKET, 1938. Common Acre were the very first winners of the Kirkland Cup in 1938. The victorious team was, back row, left to right: Albert Howe (umpire), Reg Stubbings, Tom Morton, Alec Morton and Stan Stubbings. Middle row, left to right: Sid Stubbings, Tom Summers, Jack Kerridge, Jack Stubbings and Bert Clift. Front row, left to right: Ernie Kerridge and Tom Flack. The team won the cup again in 1939, but due to losing players who went to fight the war, they sadly lost in the 1940 final, and so did not complete the hat-trick.

ISLE OF ELY SHIELD, 1925. The winning junior football team was, standing, left to right: Leslie Kerridge, Ces Gilson, Sidney Levitt and Bob Palmer. Sitting, left to right: Jack Palmer (twin to Bob), Sonny Willett, Mr Barlow (headmaster) and Stan Oakey. Cross-legged, left to right: Didi Willett (brother to Sonny), George Harwood and Congo Pettitt.

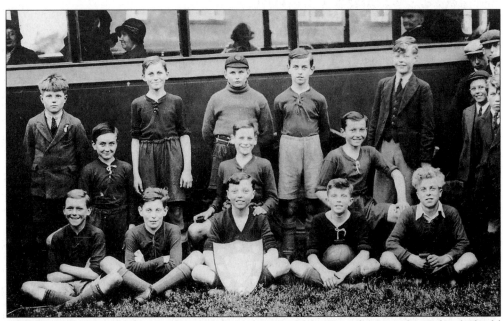

JUNIOR FOOTBALL. The Littleport School team with the Downham Market School Shield which they won for the third time, in a photograph taken in front of Washington's bus at Hilgay. The goal keeper was Howard Padget. Jack Francis and Frank Kerridge were the backs and Jim See, Roy Jordan, Fred Lincoln were the half-backs. Forwards were Doug Murfitt, Peter Rowell, Tom Sallis, Wally Gilbert and Cyril Porter.

CYCLING, 1955. Gerald Coles of East Suffolk Cycling Club leading the field in the five mile race. This was part of the cycling and athletics programme organised by the Littleport Wheelers Cycling Club as part of the annual 'Feast' at Highfield House. The Feast which also included a horticultural show and a horse show was the predecessor of the current Littleport Show.

CYCLING, 1953. The crowds watch Margaret Harwood (now Mrs Butcher) of Littleport Wheelers Cycling Club leading the race at Highfield. Laurie Hicks, club secretary is kneeling with Gordon Driver walking towards the camera and George Sewell standing behind.

CYCLING, 1954. Some of Littleport Wheelers Cycling Club, complete with cups, at the 1954 Feast. Back row, left to right: Peter Baumber, Edwin Stanley, Keith Johnson, Reg Driver, Ted Clary, Cyril Arnold, Eric Underdown, Bill Sharpe, Maurice Chilvers and Keith Dolby. Middle row, left to right: Tony Willett, Derek (Peddler) Palmer, Norman Howe and Ted Bowles. Front row, left to right: Norma Clarke, Yvonne Taylor, Poppy Easy, Margaret Harwood, Marilyn Barrett and Carol Clarke.

LITTLEPORT AND DISTRICT MOTOR CYCLE CLUB, 1950s. Scramble meetings and trials were held on the Old Bank until the early 1960s. The scrambles were very well attended, with over 5,000 spectators at the July 1958 meeting.

Three
People

INNOVATION, c. 1920. A motor cycle rickshaw in the yard at J.H. Adams shop in Main Street. Miss Doris Adams prepares for a comfortable journey behind her uncle Alf Adams.

LITTLEPORT ARMY CADETS, 1944. The Cadet Band at camp. Back row, left to right: Pat Sleight, John Hawes, Maurice Grindling, Roy Neal, Colin Thornhill, Rex Strawson and Geoffrey Hawkes. Front row: Peter Baumber, Bernard Gillett, John Ambrose, Brian Youngs, George Cooper, John Clarke, Maurice Harwood, John Newton and Les Handley.

SCHOOL PRIZEGIVING, 1932. Awards for achievement at Littleport School by both seniors and infants. The awards were made each year by Mr and Mrs Willett. Standing, left to right: Peter Rowell (watch), Mr MacGillie (?) - a friend of the Willetts, Mrs Willett, Mr Willett, Maud Moses (watch). Ronald Murfitt is seated to the left (Meccano) and on the right is Joan Bell, now Elsegood, (doll).

NEW BELLS, 1891. A new peal of bells cast by John Warner & Sons of London was hung in St George's church in 1891. The vicar, the Revd S.E. Perry MA, is seen at the church porch with the churchwardens on either side. These bells were first rung at 10 a.m. on Wednesday 24 June 1891. Through frequent ringing, the bearings became worn, and in 1935 the bells were rehung on ball bearings.

FAMILY GROUP. The Revd F.E. and Mrs Rogers with their son Tommy. The Revd Rogers was the vicar from November 1897 to February 1916. Taken from a postcard with this message under the picture: 'With our best Good-bye Wishes. May you have a spiritually Happy Christmas and a Peace-bringing New Year.'

A MODERN FIRE ENGINE IN THE 1940s. The horse-drawn engine has had pneumatic tyres and a lorry drawbar added. Members of the Volunteer Fire Brigade on the engine are, back row, left to right: Harry Shaw, Ted Rayner, Jack Barnes and Charlie South. Middle row, left to right: Geo Thurling, Bill Sparrow, Charlie Barber and Sam Clifton. At the front are Sid Barber and Jack Padgett, Doug Halls is standing on the rear.

PAST CHIEF RANGER OF THE ANCIENT ORDER OF FORESTERS. Brother William Gotobed served as the Lynn and West Norfolk District Chief Ranger in 1907. The Littleport Court 'Unity and Love', no. 2153 of the Ancient Order of Foresters, was formed in 1874, and William Gotobed became a forester in 1877. He was also a keen and active member of the Wesleyan Society. He started the firm of Gotobed & Sons in 1896, and his family are still running the business in the High Street one hundred and one years later.

GRANDSTAND. A typical viewpoint to watch the Littleport Shows of the past. Farm carts like this had benches placed on them, to form a sort of mobile grandstand. This was an early form of TV called 'travel-vision'.

MOCK BANQUET, 1934. Held in January at St John's Methodist schoolroom. In the years between the two World Wars many excuses were made for a party, and this was one of them. The same venue has been used for all the open meetings of the Littleport Society ever since its inaugural meeting there on Friday 20 March 1987.

LITTLEPORT GIRLS SCHOOL, 1928. Back row, left to right: Gladys Pettit, Winnie Hiblin, ? Butcher, Doris Baker. Third row: Gwen Easy, Edna Benton, Dora Clifton, Joyce Bell, Doris Palmer, ? Butcher, Greta Mott, Molly Murfitt. Second row: Rose Long, Lily Harley, Gladys Whitehand, Olive Chapman, ? Butcher, Queenie Thurling, Gladys Foreman, Gertie Walker, -?-, Freda Jordon. Front row: Pearl Nicholas, Lily Goodge, May Neal, Audrey Norman, Eileen Rowell, Winnie Butcher, -?-, Doris Crabb, Elsie Rodwell, -?- , Lily Rodwell, Bessie Register and Violet Rodwell.

HOPE BROTHERS CONCERT PARTY, 1933. The cast who, on 5 April 1933 performed *Ten days before the wedding*. Back row, left to right: S. Youngs, D. Saul, S. Fincham, L. Taylor, E. Smith and M. Levett. Middle row: O. Curtis, L. Sparrow, N. Gotobed, I. Lofts, S. Harrison and A. Hall. Front row: G. Butcher, E. Harrison, Miss Crabb (producer), I. Coverdale and P. Harwood.

THE FISHER'S COTTAGES, 1926. George 'Ratty' and Eliza Porter stand outside their home in the Fisher's Cottages which stood at the junction of City Road and White Hart Lane. The cottages, which were subject to frequent flooding, were believed to have been built with stone from the original thirteenth century church which stood in the village before the present building was erected in the fifteenth century. The cottages were demolished around 1937.

BLACK HORSE DROVE, 1948. The opening of the Black Horse Drove Community Centre. Major (later Sir) Harry Legge-Bourke MP, who opened the centre, is seated second from the left in the front row, and his wife is on the extreme right.

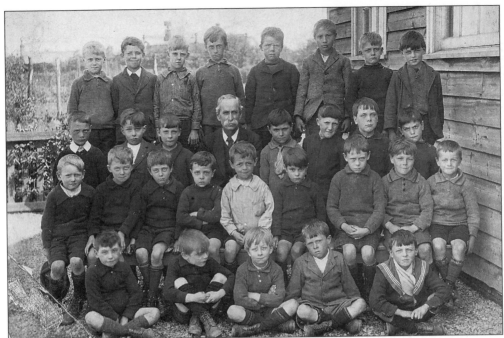

LIKELY LADS AT LITTLEPORT BOYS PRIMARY SCHOOL, 1925. In the centre of this group of boys of mixed ages, the school-teacher is 'Daddy' Verdun. The lad, with the 'cow-lick' haircut, second from the left in the second row down, is Harold Gotobed. The wooden hut on the right was the primary school-room situated to the left of the main school, and it was still in use in the 1970s. The building on the skyline was the village gas-holder.

ST JOHN AMBULANCE BRIGADE, 1938. Members of the newly re-formed brigade, which incidentally had its own ambulance in those days, are pictured in front of Mow Fen Hall with their leader Dr MacFie. Back row, left to right: Walter Fletcher, Bob Sparrow, Alf Leggett, Charlie Parker, Sid Game, Bill Cross, Ernie Coleby and J.C. Butcher. Seated, left to right: Jack Willett, Joe Gotobed, Henry Crabb, Dr MacFie, Harold Gotobed, Jim Bumpstead and W. Woodruff.

BOYS SCHOOL PLAYGROUND, 1911. Presentation of coronation medals to all scholars, and the girls have been allowed into the 'boys playground' too. All the children are seen giving 'three cheers' for King George V. The infant block, seen behind them, was in use until 1978, when it was demolished.

BIBLE CLASS, 1908. The vicar, Revd F.E. Rogers, surrounded by members of the Bible Class. The moustached man on his left is Joe Atkins, later undertaker and churchwarden. See also page 73.

WAR MEMORIAL, 1920. Capt. Colin Coote MP unveiling the memorial tablet to those who died in the First World War, at the Town Hall on the corner of Granby Street and Victoria Street on 4 December 1920.

WAR MEMORIAL, 1989. Re-dedication of the war memorial tablet on the new cenotaph at the church green on Sunday 24 September 1989. Over thirty standards were on parade including two from the USAF at Mildenhall.

THE RIOTERS. A model made for the Littleport Society by a local man in 1991. The model illustrates the story of the 1816 bread riots. The judge and the nooses for the five men sentenced to death on 22 June 1816 are suspended above the cutaway view of The Globe public house.

THE RIOTERS. This view shows the carousing inside The Globe where the trouble started on Wednesday 22 May 1816. On the extreme left is Mrs Waddelow's shop in Meader House, this was broken into and robbed during the riots.

THE VILLAGE SIGN. This was given by the Womens Institute in commemoration of their diamond jubilee in 1984. The sign is at the junction of Ponts Hill and Wellington Street and depicts, on the north side, the 1816 rioters outside The Globe public house in Main Street. Below this, is a Roman soldier representing the Roman occupation. On the south side, the church, river, railway and a windmill are depicted and beneath that, the eel gleave badge of Littleport Village College.

RIOT MEMORIAL. This stone memorial tablet to the Littleport rioters, who were executed on Friday 28 June 1816, was originally sited near their burial place. This stone was replaced with a new one in the 1980s, and the original is now in the safe keeping of the Littleport Society. Local legend says that these men were buried standing up to save space!

Four
Places

DEAR JIMMY, 1938. Views of Sandhill Bridge, the town hall, the church, the Transport Workers Union Convalescent Home at The Grange and the docks on the River Great Ouse. This postcard was sent to Glasgow by a patient at The Grange.

THE TGWU CONVALESCENT HOME IN THE 1930s. Now The Grange nursing home, in Grange Lane. Union members were allowed two weeks of convalescence. The change-over day was Monday, and each week approximately half of the patients would leave to be replaced by newcomers.

SURPRISE, SURPRISE. The new Monday arrivals for The Grange were met each week by staff and patients in fancy dress. This group was known as 'MacNamara's Band' and would wait in Grange Lane while the bus from the station bearing the new residents was stopped by a bogus police officer outside the Plough and Harrow public house in Ely Road.

TWO PLOUGH AND HARROWS IN 1934. The new public house rises behind the old in Ely Road. The landlord, Arthur Townsend, stands in the doorway, where the sign says 'Please use back door for shop'. There is a small sweet shop on the south (righthand) end. The new pub had a shop at the north end.

Ely Road, Littleport.

ELY ROAD, 1930s. This view near Highfield House, which is on the left, is one of five taken from a lettercard produced by Butchers of Main Street. Another of these views is on page 54. The large black shed near the house on the right of the picture was used as the ticket office for the annual Littleport Show.

MILLPIT, ELY ROAD, 1915. There is some discussion as to what exactly was the 'mill' which is referred to here, corn grinding, a saw mill or indeed was the whole area a marl pit? This stretch of road was formerly called Mill End, and a windmill is shown on Samuel Wells' map of the Bedford Level dated 1828, but this was some distance away, and probably situated in Millfield or Mill Close (now The Crescent).

ARBERS MILL, 1900. Along Ten Mile Bank this was a corn-grinding mill sited almost on the actual river bank. It was probably the last working mill in Littleport, and it was certainly the last mill to be demolished. This occurred in December 1952, and it was believed to have stood on that site for over one hundred years. See also page 22.

GRANBY STREET, 1925. This small street was, at that time, part of the main road between Cambridge and Kings Lynn. This view is looking north towards Wellington Street and Ferry Lane (now Station Road). The Marquis of Granby on the left has changed from an inn to a hotel, see also page 56.

THE TOWN HALL, 1930. This was erected in 1879 by Littleport builder William Drake at a cost of £1,198. Originally a vestry and a public hall, this is now a public library, the offices of the parish council, and also of the Town Lands Charity who own these premises.

THE HOLMES, 1910. This area is situated on the north side of City Road. The land on the left (west) side of The Holmes road is owned by the Town Lands Charity. The old cottages shown here were replaced by new bungalows by 1969.

THE HOLMES, c. 1960. A sign-board formerly on the end of one of the old cottages, proclaimed: 'Notice. Any person occupying a house belonging to the Feoffees, and having children, is hereby cautioned against allowing such children to be an annoyance to their neighbours, either by assembling in groups and using unbecoming language, or in any other way disturbing the peace of their neighbours. And every occupier is required to keep his or her house and garden clean and in neat order. And is also admonished to attend Divine Service (unless prevented by illness), at least once on every Lord's Day, any person neglecting to comply herewith will be liable to immediate notice to quit. By Order of the Feoffees. Dated 21 March 1865.' It is rather amusing to think that in all probability none of the residents at that time could read the notice anyway!

46

PONTS HILL PUMP, sometime before 1910. The large tree on the left of the road is on the site of the present Ex-servicemens Club. Clearly this pump is for 'bucket use only', but many other pumps were on brick stands to facilitate the filling of water carts and carriers.

THE HYTHE PUMP, sometime before 1914. These pumps were for public use, and there was one situated in many of the village streets. Larger houses often had their own private water pump. Some of the pumps had a type of filter, but even that could not guarantee pure water which was free from insects and other obnoxious particles. A piped supply of fresh water eventually arrived in the village in July 1924.

WIND AND STEAM, early 1900s. A steam locomotive passes in front of Canhams smock windmill and on through the station. Littleport station is on the Ely to Kings Lynn railway line which was opened in 1847, and which was electrified in 1991.

REDUNDANT MILL, 1912. This mill, known as Canham's mill, situated near the station became redundant and was sold to J. Ivatt Sallis for 12 10s 0d on 5 June 1912. It was demolished twenty days later!

A NEW STRAW HAT. A barn, not unlike the village Tithe Barn, under preparation for re-thatching in the 1930s. Out of this apparent chaos will emerge a neatly thatched roof. The pole carrying the overhead electricity cables reminds us that electricity first came to Littleport in 1934.

THE TYTHE BARN, c. 1920. This stood on Parsons Lane then a rough track which was repaired with stones. The first houses were built in Parsons Lane just prior to the Second World War. The barn was burned down by accident on 10 November 1945 and was not rebuilt. Much of the area was used when Parsons Lane was widened, and the bungalows of Tythe Court were built on the remainder.

ST GEORGES, 1930. The parish church seen from the south. Many of the gravestones shown in this view were removed in 1980 to facilitate grass cutting and the general tidying of the graveyard, which had become rather an eyesore. A survey had previously been made by pupils of Littleport Village College in 1976, and a schedule of tombstones and monuments was produced. The Church Register records date from 1599.

INSIDE ST GEORGE'S. This interior view shows the large stained glass east window. There is a tortoise stove where now stands the lectern, and the large stone font on the left has since been moved to the south aisle. The Union Flag is no longer in evidence. The building is mainly fifteenth century, however, it was enlarged by the addition of a north nave and aisle in 1857.

St. Georges Church, Littleport

Wishing you a bright
and Happy Christmas.

Greetings.

HAPPY CHRISTMAS, 1914. A Christmas greetings card featuring views of the parish church of Saint George. The greetings card industry has developed rather alarmingly since those days! Note that the tower clock was square faced, this was replaced in 1919 by the round faced clock, shown opposite, as a memorial to those villagers who lost their lives in the Great War. The fourteenth century tower is the oldest part of the church.

THE VICARAGE, sometime before 1892. Immediately next door to the church, the Revd Ferris was the last curate to live in this 'old' vicarage. It's successor was built by Messrs Porter & Son of Southery, and that new vicarage was occupied by Revd S.E. Perry MA on 30 August 1892. The 'new' building is now a residential home known as 'The Old Vicarage', and yet another new vicarage was built in the 1980s. Between 1855 and 1892 the parish vicar lived in The Grange, see page 42. The earliest vicar whose name has been recorded was Michael in 1250.

Wesleyan Church, Littleport.

THE METHODIST CHURCH. In Littleport, people called Methodists began meeting firstly in a cottage in Crown Lane until a small church was built in 1806 in the area then known as Mill End, now called High Street. This chapel had no heating and was lit by candles. The growth of the society was such that their chapel had to be enlarged in 1835 with a new frontage and side balconies. In 1889 there was the stone laying of a fine Gothic church that was completed in 1890 at a total cost of £1,600. This building seated 275 on the ground floor and 100 in the balcony. Heating by means of water pipes was a great innovation at that time. A pipe organ was installed in 1909, pumped by hand until an electric blower was installed in 1938. This church, on the left of the earlier chapel, is used for present day worship and the original chapel is used for Sunday school work and midweek meetings. The photograph shows the then Wesleyan church, sometime around 1906.

HIGH STREET, *c.* 1920. A photograph viewed towards the south of the street, showing both new and old churches.

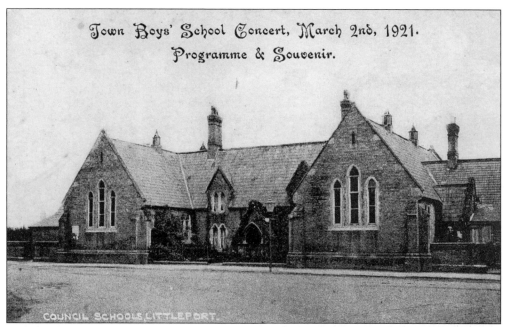

Town Boys' School Concert, March 2nd, 1921.
Programme & Souvenir.

COUNCIL SCHOOLS LITTLEPORT.

TOWN BOYS SCHOOL, 2 March 1921. This picture appears on a postcard, overprinted on the other side with the Boys' School entertainment programme. It appears to have been an early 'black and white minstrels show' because the second half includes a list of 'niggers' which surely would be most offensive these days.

HIGH STREET, 1898. Spooner's Stores, at No. 6 was later to become Burtons, and more recently Fine Fare. Subsequently it reverted to private ownership before becoming unoccupied in the early 1990s. These buildings are immediately next door to the Methodist church premises shown opposite. See also page 71.

WOOD FEN. At 4.00 a.m. on 18 May 1891, the snow suggests that winter was very late that year. The thick hedgerows have long disappeared from this area.

WOOD FEN, 1925. This is taken from a lettercard of five views (also mentioned on page 43). Most of the trees, which gave this area its name, have long ago succumbed to age, to the axe, and to Dutch elm disease. Fortunately in recent years there has been a programme of new tree planting here and in other parts of the village.

FRIAR'S NINE. This lane has not suffered quite so much from deforestation, and some trees and hedges still remain, although it is nothing like this picture shows. The unusual name is thought to come from the legend that nine friars were on their way from Ely to Walsingham (in Norfolk) when they were murdered and then buried in this area.

NEW ROAD, LITTLEPORT. NO. 16.

NEW ROAD, c. 1900. This followed the north bank of the Old Croft River, it was a continuation of Silt Road, and both of these roads are believed to be part of the original path along the riverside.

GRANBY STREET, *c*. 1900. Looking northwards, the Town Hall doorway is on the right. The Marquis of Granby inn closed in the 1960s and is now a local authority hostel.

GRANBY STREET, 1920s. Looking southwards this is clearly a street of many traders. The shapes of the dwellings on both sides of this highway have changed dramatically during the passing years, but it is still second only to Main Street with its number of shops.

OLD SHOPS, STATION ROAD. Harringtons Agricultural Merchant and Percy Crabb's barbers shop with its pole, were at Nos. 9 and 11. Not far away from The George and Dragon public house, which was the scene of some incidents during the Littleport Riots of 1816, see pages 39 and 40.

Factory Lane and Ferry Lane, Littleport, (showing Hope Bros. Factory)

CHANGING NAMES. Factory Lane and Ferry Lane, are now White Hart Lane and Station Road. This corner was the site of frequent floods, see page 92. Hope Bros. Factory can be seen in the background, and the station is still operational although unmanned. The Ferry and The White Hart have long since disappeared.

MAIN STREET, *c.* 1900. Looking west along the north side. The white building just left of centre is Meader House, already owned by Lloyds Bank. Immediately before Meader House is The Globe public house (now the Co-op stores), whilst just visible beyond it is The Crown, which remains almost unaltered.

MAIN STREET, looking west along the south side. The saddlers shop on the immediate left was Defews at No.7. Next to this, at No.9, was Heygates drapers shop, followed, at No.11, by Cragg's butchers shop (now Barclays bank). Beyond that was the eighteenth century home of the Adam's family at No.13, and this at one time housed the village post office.

MAIN STREET, looking eastwards, sometime before 1919. The Granby Inn and Town Hall are at the end of the road, the white building is Wrights, saddler and harnessmaker, see also page 72. The postcard, which is dated 24 August 1919 states 'Just a card to let you know I will be arriving at 7.12 tomorrow evening'. That shows great faith in the postal and rail services!

VICTORIA STREET, between 1900 and 1910. Looking eastwards, we can see Cornelius (Connie) Cawthorn's general stores on the left at No.13. The iron railings, immediately next door, are in front of the former Primitive Methodist church, which, following its closure in the 1960s, was converted into flats, Nos. 15 and 17. A stone in the wall at the rear was 'Laid by M.J. Dennis, 26 July 1871'.

MAIN STREET. A photograph viewed from Crown Corner at the turn of the century. It shows Meader House still as a private residence, with its garden opposite behind the railings containing some very tall trees.

MAIN STREET FROM CROWN CORNER, 1955. Showing the pseudo-Tudor building of Lloyds bank on the site of Meader House which was demolished in the 1930s. Beyond that The Globe inn can be seen, which was demolished in 1962, and which was the meeting place of the Rioters in 1816. See also pages 39 and 40.

AUDLEY HOUSE. This imposing mansion had its frontage on Church Lane, and extended almost to the Crown Lane corner. It was the twenty roomed Georgian residence of the Luddington family who were local farmers and landowners. The garden of this property was enclosed by a high wall, and comprised almost the entire block bordered by Church Lane, Wellington Street and Crown Lane, an area of nearly one and a half acres. The main 'carriage' entrance was at the corner opposite the former primary school in Wisbech Road.

A FIREPLACE IN AUDLEY HOUSE. This building was sold on Thursday 28 November 1929, and it was demolished soon after. The present Audley Garage was erected on part of the site, and it was opened for business in October 1933 by Henry John Fuller.

THE RAILWAY STATION at the turn of the century. If you look carefully on the platform you can see a penny farthing bicycle, a one-legged porter, and the station master whose name was Mr Green.

SANDHILL RAILWAY CROSSING, 1958. Pictured on the left are the site offices of Derek Crouch Ltd., who were engaged in Great Ouse River improvements; in the centre is the railway gate-keeper's cottage, which was demolished in the 1980s; and on the right is The Black Horse public house, which is also shown on pages 93 and 95 in different conditions.

Five
Workers

WOMEN ON ASSEMBLY LINES AT HOPE BROTHERS, *c.* 1930. Girls started work here from the age of fourteen, and about sixty worked on this top floor making shirts and pyjamas. The factory manager on the left is Frank Smith, and the forewoman standing right of centre is Mary Ann Barber.

THE SHIRT FACTORY. The inset is Thomas Peacock, a native of Littleport, who had become a merchant shipper trading from China. On his return to England he decided to start a retail enterprise which would give value for money by keeping its prices as low as possible. Contemporary traders laughed at the idea, but in 1874 Thomas Peacock opened his first small shop on Ludgate Hill in the City of London. The firm was called 'Hope Brothers' - an exhortation to its employees. Success brought expansion to other shops and within a year or two Thomas Peacock opened his first factory to cut out the middleman. This was a large three floored building in Littleport. The factory made shirts and collars and completely changed the conditions of life for the women in the village. From toil and hardship working on the land for a pittance, the women now had a new, well paid, form of labour. Working conditions were good and a social life was fully catered for. A club was established and a clubhouse providing a piano, games, a writing room and a well-stocked library. This was Alexandra Hall in Victoria Street which is now flats. Tennis courts and croquet lawns were laid out in the grounds, now No. 22-26 Barkhams Lane, and the several hundred employees lead happy and healthy lives.

FIRST FLOOR SMILES FROM THE GIRLS, *c.* 1950. They are making collars, trimmings for cuffs, and neckbands, in addition to white, blue and pin-striped shirts, and striped pyjamas.

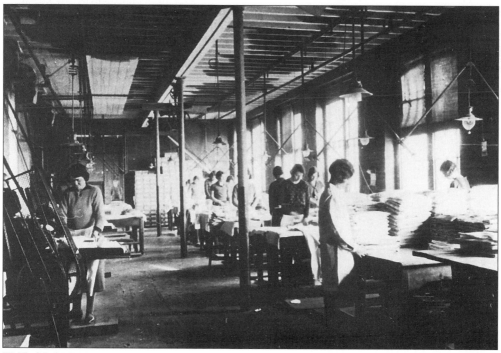

THE GROUND FLOOR LAUNDRY, 1930. New shirts and pyjamas were pressed, and dress shirts were also starched. In the 1930s, household laundry was also done for a fee, 'in by Monday ready by Friday'.

RUSH HOUR IN VICTORIA STREET, postmarked 1906. All the girls are walking, but by 1925 the majority were using bicycles, because many of them came in from the surrounding fens. In later years, some of them arrived by bus from as far afield as Downham Market.

INSIDE ALEXANDRA HALL, HOPE BROS. GIRLS' CLUB. This was open every evening except Sunday from 6.00 pm until 9.00 pm. Strictly 'girls only', including the Friday night dances, but on that evening the girls would be met outside by a row of fellows! In addition to the library, whose shelves are seen at the back, and various games, there were four bathrooms which the girls could use for a small fee, but towels were not provided!

LITTLEPORT DOCKS, 1900. A barge loaded with hay is transferred to rail. The hay grown around Southery, Norfolk was transported along the Great Ouse River and then sent by train to London. The station horse, on the extreme left, was one of two that were housed in stables beyond the building on the right.

JOE LOFTS, 1919. Joe ran the station bus and is shown delivering fish to Ernie Crabb and his mother at No.19 Wellington Street, the horse-drawn bus is behind them. The fish would have come off the train, probably from King's Lynn. Joe's fleet of vehicles expanded in later years to include a taxi and two minibuses.

TOM SMITH'S GARAGE, *c.* 1920. The man on the left is Frank Manthorpe, and his companion is Mick Smith. Situated at No.16 Main Street, the garage was subsequently owned by Mr Morris and then H. John Fuller, who moved the business to Audley Garage in 1933, see page 61. A fish and chip shop was built on the forecourt by the Snushall Family, (see also page 12), later owned by John Fletcher, who also kept and bred mink in the garage building. The last 'chipper' was Arthur Smith who fried the final fish there in 1968.

THE BREWERY, 1895. This was on the Granby Street junction with City Road. The brewery was owned by W. Cutlack, brewer and spirit merchant (later to become Hall, Cutlack and Harlock). The brewery house, on the right, is still standing at No.6 Granby Street and it has been converted into flats, but the rest of the buildings were demolished in 1963.

MARATHON RUNNER, 1920s. Mr E.V. Norman's Foden 'Neddy' at Will Harwood's blacksmiths forge, Littleport Bridge. This lorry took the first steam powered lorryload of potatoes from Littleport to London. The round trip took four days and nights as boiler tube leaks dowsing the fire necessitated repairs at Harlow. Will Harwood is on the left and Ernie Cooper on the extreme right. Tingay Norman, the driver, sat with one leg outside the cab because of the restricted space.

HORSELESS CARRIAGE, late 1920s. Mr E.V. Norman's Foden steam lorry unloading 'mids' meal at Goddard & Peake's granary at No.3 Wellington Street. Standing on the lorry are, left to right: Alf King, Bertram 'Sonny' Peake and Ted Norman. Horace Watson is in the doorway of the granary.

MR A. MACKENDER OUTSIDE HIS SHOE REPAIR SHOP. Situated between No.s 4 and 6 High Street, the window of Mackender's shop contains a great deal of football equipment, and the back room of the premises was used as a club room by local footballers.

CORONATION WEEK, 1953. Burtons Store at No.6 High Street won the decorated window competition. In the doorway are, left to right: Arthur Chambers (manager) and Ron Barber, who later became manager of the Fine Fare store on the same site until his retirement.

WENDING HIS WEARY WAY! Mr Jim Sparrow shown in Main Street on his way home from his straw and chaff business in Hempfield Road in the 1920s.

THE DINKIE CHINA SHOP, *c.* 1920. The proprietors were Barker and Gotobed at the time of this photograph. The shop was at number No.12 Main Street, standing in the doorway on the right is the manageress Miss Barrett (later Mrs Lizzie Myhill) and her assistant Miss Martin.

BUTCHER'S CART, early 1900s. This is one of several roundsmen who travelled the area visiting the droves in the Fens. Although the cart was primitive it was the mode of salesmen in those days.

SADDLER'S SHOP, MAIN STREET. Mr Albert Wright, centre, proudly displays his work at No.3 Main Street. All the harnesses on show were made for a single order from Hubert Cooke in 1913. The premises are still owned by the Wright family, the saddlery and tarpaulin business closed recently.

JOE ATKINS, CARPENTER OF LITTLEPORT, 1902. Joe is pictured with the first cart he made. He became the local undertaker between the two Great Wars, his name is remembered by Atkins Close the new road alongside the cemetery (see also page 37).

FENLAND FARM, 1920s. A tumbril used for muck spreading on H. Kerridge's farm in Hale Fen. The Kerridge's used only Suffolk Punch horses for work on their farm. Normally only one horse would be required for this particular task, but in winter conditions sometimes two would be needed.

CELERY GROWING IN THE FENS, 1950s. Two ladies transplant seedlings into the nursery bed during April. The plants are grown on until June when they are transferred to the fields to be planted by a 'Robot Planter' at approximately 20,000 plants per acre. Celery, which was harvested during December, was once a common sight in the black fenland fields, but sadly the preference for washed, packed produce caused the demise of 'proper' celery.

ROBOT PLANTER AND HIS TEAM!

Men till the fields at Littleport,
The spreading fields and low;
And as they toil, amid the soil
I wonder if they know
That where they drop the yellow grain
An ocean used to flow;
And little ships to little quays
Came gladly after tossing seas,
And sailors laughed and took their ease,
Long, long ago.

Men till the fields at Littleport,
I wonder if they stir
Amid the stones, the crumpled bones
Of some old seafarer;
And feel the salt tang on their lips
Of winds that used to blow;
Or hear across a vanished bay
Old sailor chanties softly gay,
From dust of those who went their way
Long, long ago.

When evenings close on Littleport,
I wonder if the tide
From distant Lynn comes surging in,
And giant vessels ride
Against the little cottage panes;
And ruby lanterns glow
On slender masts that throng the sea
From Shippea Hill to Southery;
And all is as it used to be
Long, long ago.

Elizabeth Fleming.

The author of the poem was born around 1900 on a farm in Falkirk Scotland, and moved with her family to Henny Farm near Soham in the 1920s. She was run over by a horse and cart as a child, and remained a cripple for the rest of her life, which ended in about 1978. One of her brothers, Duncan Fleming, who was a pilot in the First World War, lived at No.12 Wellington Street, Littleport until his death in the late 1980s. She wrote several books and at least one play, and this poem was first published in *Punch* magazine on 20 May 1925. It has been set to music by the late Catherine Browning, the first wife of the late Bob Browning, a Founder Member and former Chairman of The Littleport Society. If Littleport ever declares U.D.I. this will surely be our National Anthem!

FEN LAND FARM, 1930s. Drilling sugar beets on Rains Farms, Ten Mile Bank, using a Smythe four-row drill. The use of multi-germ seed produced many plants in thick rows which had to be 'chopped out' with a hand hoe and then each group of plants would be 'singled' to one by hand. Sugar beets are white roots related to beetroots. It was not until the middle of the eighteenth century that it was discovered how to extract sugar from sugar beets. The industry was not established until the nineteenth century, but now over half the world's sugar comes from sugar beets. The crops grown locally are sent to nearby factories at Wissington, Bury St Edmunds or Kings Lynn for processing.

DRILLING CONTINUES, WITH A CLEAR SIGNAL!

HARVEST SCENE, USING A REAPER, *c.* 1920. These are two typical scenes on H. Kerridge's farm in Hale Fen. Since pre-historic times, corn was cut by hand using a tool made from bone or wood, with a sharp piece of flint attached. From this developed the sickle, made from iron, and used in Roman times. At this time, the scythe was also developed, and is still in use on farms today. The first mechanical reaper was made in 1826, and from this developed the reaper-binder at the end of the ninteenth century. After the corn had been cut it was placed in stooks of six or eight sheaves, which were stood against each other to dry, before it was placed in stacks or in barns for storage, prior to threshing. Both the reaper-binder and the thresher were superseded by the combine harvester, which was originally pulled by a tractor. These machines are now driven by their own engine.

HARVEST SCENE, USING A REAPER-BINDER, *c.* 1920.

TYTHE YARD, c. 1910. This could easily have been part of the vicar's income in the years up to 1839! The load is delivered by Charlie Ayres in the yard behind the Tythe Barn. If you look very carefully, you can see the parish church through the branches of the trees just above the cart load.

STACKING SHEAVES OF WHEAT. The elevator is powered by the horse turning a rig. The building in the background is Littleport railway station. The corn was threshed in the winter and the grain transferred to the nearby mill to be ground.

CORN STACKS, 1950s. Once a common sight in the Fens the stacks would be thatched with straw to keep the corn dry. Each stack was usually built in a day and would contain the crop from 8-10 acres. The thatcher was kept supplied with straw by his 'server'. Jack Oakey, who was employed as a thatcher by Mr J.E. Kerridge, became three-times winner of the Isle of Ely Thatching Championship.

CHAMPION THATCHER. Jack Oakey with his trophies.

BUSH FARM, 1950s. The Kerridge family harvesting potatoes using Nuffield tractors. This was in the early days of mechanisation, formerly the crop would have been picked by hand. When one considers that the potato originated in the highlands of the Andes mountains in South America, it seems strange that it grows so very well in our Fenland village. This crop was introduced to Europe in the sixteenth century, and by the middle of the eighteenth century it had become the main food for most people, replacing their staple diet of bread.

FIELD UNDERDRAINING, 1956. Mr John Rains oversees the laying of clay 'underdrains' on his farm, a necessary operation to prevent low-lying farmland from becoming waterlogged. The pipes would be placed in the bottom of the trench, normally just above the clay bed, flowing into fieldside dykes.

Six
Rivers and Floods

FLOODS AT LITTLEPORT, 1915. The railway embankment is the only land in sight.

FENLAND RIVER SCENE, in the late 1950s. Seen during the flood prevention works, this view is from the west bank looking along Ten Mile Bank towards Norfolk. A tug with a string of barges is heading towards Littleport, and the Forresters Arms on the main road is just visible above the tug. Note how the water in the river is much higher than the farmland.

A TIGHT FIT, *c.* 1898. Mr E.H. Gooby manoeuvring his barges under Sandhill Bridge whilst onlookers watch from the bridge. His son Harold is seen kneeling with his pet dog. The man standing on the jetty is thought to be the landlord of the Black Horse public house, to the left of the bridge. The ducks moved during the photographic time exposure which has made them blurred.

82

SANDHILL WOODEN BRIDGE. This was constructed in 1829-30 and carried a single carriageway over the Great Ouse River at the end of Victoria Street. The sketch shows a view looking across the river to the Black Horse public house. This bridge stood for over sixty years.

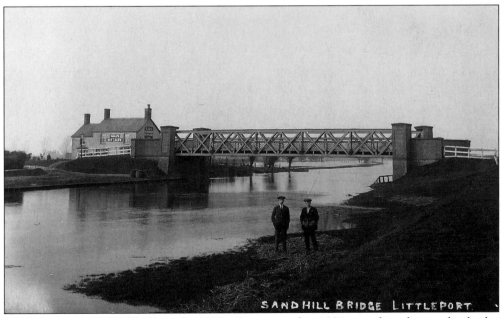

SANDHILL IRON BRIDGE, in the 1920s. Constructed in 1894 to replace the wooden bridge the new bridge was wider and carried two lanes of traffic. This view shows that there was no high flood bank on the Littleport side of the river. Through the bridge, water can be seen on the Moors.

SANDHILL IRON BRIDGE. Seen from the north, shortly before its demolition in 1958. It had served the village well for sixty-four years. The concrete bridge which replaced it is shown below.

SANDHILL CONCRETE BRIDGE, 1959. The current bridge was built as part of the Flood Prevention Scheme which started in the late 1950s. The contractor responsible for straightening and deepening the Great Ouse River was Derek Crouch Ltd. who had their site office in Padnal, shown on page 62. The Great Ouse River Board provided a chain punt as a pedestrian ferry while the bridge was under construction.

RIVER TRAFFIC, *c.* 1920. Mr E.H. Gooby's barges moored near Littleport Bridge. The barges just visible on the far bank beyond the bridge are loaded with road 'clunch' brought from Isleham. There is a pony and trap crossing the bridge.

LITTLEPORT IRON BRIDGE, in the late 1950s. Built in 1873 this bridge, with a clear span of one hundred and five feet, carried the main A10 road over the Great Ouse River in line with the Mildenhall road. In the 1950s, gas lamps were still in use on the bridge. The iron bridge was replaced between 1974-75 by a new concrete structure to align with the new A10 Littleport bypass.

THE WEST BANK, *c.* 1925. Cottages near the docks between the bridges viewed from the east bank of the river. There are no garages but there are boats tied up to the bank for emergency use.

RIVER GREAT OUSE IN FLOOD, 1915. The same cottages viewed from the rear, now surrounded with water. The boats are needed now to go anywhere, even to visit the stack which is surrounded by water. The larger house still exists.

NANCY, 1930. Unloading sacks of grain from Henry Banhams barge *Nancy* which worked the Great Ouse River between Cambridge and Kings Lynn.

DOCKS AND RAILWAY QUAY. This view of the docks looking towards the properties on the facing page alongside the Great Ouse River, shows a railway wagon with a load already taken from a barge.

CROFT RIVER. Looking towards Littleport Bridge from the docks. The Croft River is the original course of the Ouse, discharging into the sea at Wisbech, formerly called Ousebeach.

STATION ROAD AND THE HOLMES LODE. Looking towards the railway station, this part of the former Croft River flows from the docks through a culvert under the railway line. It was widened in about 1882 to supply Hope Bros. factory with water, and to provide an additional source for villagers.

THE FROZEN GREAT OUSE RIVER, JANUARY 1963. There are several people on the ice near Sandhill Bridge. The river was frozen solid for about five weeks, and many a dare was laid by motor-cyclists to see who could travel the furthest along it. Some were even known to use this slippery route to get to work.

FLOODS, JANUARY 1915. This view from Station Road towards The Holmes, shows the Holmes Lode in flood. The postcard was sent 'With love from Willie to Daddy, wishing you many happy returns of your Birthday'. It seems a strange choice of picture!

FLOODS NEAR THE STATION. Railway wagons stand idle in one of the many floods at the turn of the century. The line of the Holmes Lode is completely lost. Canhams Mill shown on the left, was 'lost' in June 1912, as detailed on page 48.

THE MOORS FROM STATION ROAD. This is believed to be the floods of 1928. The signal box in the centre background marks the end of the railway goods yard. The flood bank of the Great Ouse River is clearly visible, but obviously proved quite useless!

A FLOODED STATION ROAD, 1947. Seen from the station yard, there are several vehicles on the road, and the Holmes Lode is full to the brim. In the foreground is a lorry load of sandbags, brought to try to stem the flow.

A FLOODED STATION ROAD, 1928. The sandbags are already in position near Quay Hill. Hope Bros. 'shirt factory' can be clearly seen on the sky line, it is one of the three highest buildings in the centre of the village. The boys viewing the scene include 'Smut' Smith, Chris Lee, and Bill Barber.

FLOODS, 1937. The junction of White Hart Lane and Station Road, with the butchers shop of W.H. Cox. At the highest tide, the water in the shop was at least six inches deep, and all the electrical equipment was put out of order.

FLOODS, 1947. The same sorry scene just ten years later than the previous photograph. The light coloured building in the centre, is the Gospel Hall in City Road, and it is clearly visible following the demolition, some ten years earlier, of the Fisher's Cottages mentioned on page 35.

FLOODS, MARCH 1937. These cottages are in Station Road, which runs straight along the front of the picture, at the end of the railings. Mrs Ward lived here, and she was well known for 'calling her ducks home' each evening from the river, and they would waddle along behind her. However on this occasion they could swim all the way!

FLOODS AT SANDHILL BRIDGE, MARCH 1937. When the Great Ouse River was flowing at its normal level, the gap between it and the bridge was twenty-five feet. The buildings, shown on the extreme right, were bathing huts, and they stood on a lawn.

FLOODS, 8 JANUARY 1928. The scene at Beaconsfield Terrace Nos.13-27 City Road, with the Fisher's Cottages in the background. The wagon in the centre of the flood has planks resting on either side, to enable residents of the Terrace to walk from their front walls onto dry land, without getting their feet wet.

FLOODS, 1937. Showing that the railway line towards Cambridge is on slightly higher ground. The signal box, in the centre, at the end of the goods sidings is mentioned on page 90.

AERIAL VIEW OF THE FLOODS, 1947. This shows the great devastation that water can cause. The Great Ouse River on the right has clearly broken its bank. The road leads from the Sandhill Bridge on the right, over the level crossing, and into Victoria Street, with the dwellings in the middle of the picture. The triangular area to the top left is The Moors, which can be seen in happier days on pages 22 to 24. Areas of land such as the 17,000 acres of the parish of Littleport, which are near or even below sea level, are under constant threat from flooding. It happened fifty years ago, and several times in the last hundred years, who can say that it will never happen again?

Acknowledgements

The Littleport Society wishes to acknowledge the kind help of the Central Library, Lion Yard, Cambridge for providing photographs and information from 'The Cambridgeshire Collection'.

The following members and friends of the Society also provided photographs and information: Ron Barber, Mrs I. Bent, Graham Butcher, Pam Chase, Gordon Chase, the late Mrs Ruth Crabb, Reg Driver, R. Gooby, James Hupp (for the Hupp Collection), the late Doris Kerridge, Peter Kerridge, Stephen Kerridge, Staff at Littleport Leisure, Heber Martin, Ron Murfitt, Roy Neal, David Newstead, Ron Norman, Jack Oakey, David Palmer, The parish church, Roger Rudderham, Mrs E.M. Scott, the late Jack Taylor, Andy Wright.

Committee members of The Littleport Society who gave very generous assistance are (in alphabetic order): Ivan Coussell, Bruce Frost, Grenville Goodson, Margaret Goodson, Harold Gotobed, Ray Hodson, Elliott Kerridge, Jean Peachey, David Porter, Joyce Rawkins, Derek Richings, Crawford Smith, Dennis Thurling.

Books consulted include:
Barber's Littleport & District Directory & Almanack (various years editions)
Chronicles of Littleport, R.T. Sonley
Old Littleport, Roger I. Rudderham